"Rejoice!"

The Nativity of our Lord Jesus Christ

*Illustrated in watercolors for Children and Adults, with references
from the Holy Scriptures from the Orthodox Study Bible.*

Written and Illustrated by
Maria Athanasiou

DEDICATION

To my family:

Elizabeth, Dean, Nicholas, Marisa, Anastasia, Gregory, Peter, Denise, Kristina, Evan, Petey, Zoe, Andrew, Kathryn, Alexandra, and Andrew.

I would like to thank my grandchildren Nicholas, Marisa and Anastasia Soteropoulos for their valuable suggestions and for organizing with me the artwork and the pages. It was great fun and precious memories.

I would like to acknowledge and thank Rev. Father Sarantis Loulakis, Rev. Father Nicholas Soteropoulos, Rev. Father Dimitrios Moraitis and Rev. Father Konstantinos Kalogridis.

Glory to God for all things.

Copyright © 2009 by Maria Athanasiou
Library of Congress Control Number: 2009907462
ISBN: Softcover 978-1-4415-5810-7
Hardcover 978-1-4415-7497-8
E-Book 978-1-4771-6732-8

Print information available on the last page

Rev. date: 06/04/2015

To order additional copies of this book, contact:
Xlibris
1-888-795-4274
www.Xlibris.com
Orders@Xlibris.com

JERUSALEM IN JUDEA

Jerusalem and the Mount of Olives beyond the walls, with the Garden of Gethsemane.

Before the Birth of Jesus, Judea was ruled by the Roman Empire led by Caesar. Herod was a Roman governor that Caesar had sent to Judea, who governed from 37 B.C until 4 A.D. He was a very cruel man and though he himself was not a Jew he called himself king of Judea.

The Jewish people were without a kingdom for centuries and they were suffering under the Roman rulers. They were praying to God to send them someone to free them and save them, like He had sent Moses in the past. They were anxiously waiting for their Savior. They called Him the Messiah.

Messiah is the Mediator between God and the world and comes from the Greek word Mesias.

THE TEMPLE IN JERUSALEM

In the Temple of Jerusalem, which was built by king Solomon, was a Priest named Zacharias. He was married to Elizabeth and they were both righteous people and loved God above all.

They were both praying to God for a child, but they had no children, and they had reached a very old age. They were very sad that they had no child, but they were still devoted and faithful to God.

There was in the days of Herod, the king of Judea, a certain priest named Zacharias, of the division of Abijah. His wife was of the daughters of Aaron, and her name was Elizabeth. They were both righteous before God, walking in all the commandments and ordinances of the Lord blameless. But they had no child, because Elizabeth was barren and they were both advanced in years. Luke 1:5-7

ZACHARIAS IN THE TEMPLE

One day when Zacharias was inside the Temple offering burnt sacrifices to God on the Altar, an angel of the Lord appeared in front of him and Zacharias became greatly afraid.

But the angel said to him, "Do not be afraid, Zacharias, for your prayer is heard; and your wife Elizabeth will bear you a son, and you shall call his name John. Luke 1:13

Then Zacharias asked the angel, how this could happen, that they can have a child in their old age.

THE VISION OF ZACHARIAS

And the angel answered and said to him, "I am Gabriel, who stands in the presence of God and was sent to speak to you and bring you these glad tidings. But behold you will be mute and not be able to speak until the day these things take place, because you did not believe my words, which will be fulfilled in their own time". Luke 1:19-20

The angels are God's messengers. They are heavenly spirits, without solid bodies. They are invisible but they can take different forms according to God's commands. In heaven they serve and praise God always. The angels are sent by God to protect us and they act very fast to do the will of God.

WITH GOD NOTHING IS IMPOSSIBLE

Saint Elizabeth was called barren because she had no children. Barren women were seen by the Jews of that time as having no favor with God and it was very shameful to be barren. Yet, Elizabeth and Zacharias continued to pray to God and trust in Him.

God blessed Elizabeth with a child in her old age and made her a joyful mother. For with God nothing will be impossible. Luke 1:37

God is always near and hears our prayers.

ANNUNCIATION

When Elizabeth was six months with child, the archangel Gabriel was sent from God to Nazareth, a city of Galilee, to Mary a young Virgin, who was engaged to be married to Joseph, an honest and righteous carpenter. Mary was Elizabeth's cousin.

And having come in, the angel said to her, "Rejoice highly favored one, the Lord is with you; blessed are you among women!" But when she saw him, she was troubled at his saying, and considered what manner of greeting this was. Then the angel said to her, "Do not be afraid, Mary, for you have found favor with God. And behold, you will conceive in your womb and bring forth a Son, and shall call His name JESUS. He will be great, and will be called the Son of the Highest; and the Lord God will give Him the throne of His father David. Luke 1:28-32

JESUS SON OF THE HIGHEST

Then Mary said to the angel, "How can this be, since I do not know a man?" And the angel answered and said to her, "The Holy Spirit will come upon you, and the power of the Highest will overshadow you; therefore, also that Holy One who is to be born will be called the Son of God. Now indeed, Elizabeth your relative has also conceived a son in her old age; and this is now the sixth month for her who was called barren. For with God nothing will be impossible." Then Mary said, "Behold the maidservant of the Lord! Let it be to me according to your word." And the angel departed from her. Luke 1:34-38

Mary trusted the Lord with all her heart, and agreed to give birth to Jesus Christ and so gladly do the will of God. She is blessed among women. When we seek to do the will of God, we also receive His blessings.

THE VIRGIN MARY VISITS SAINT ELIZABETH

When Mary learned that her cousin Elizabeth was expecting a child, she left for the hill country of Judah, where Elizabeth lived, to visit her. Elizabeth was very glad when she saw Mary and she felt her baby leap in her womb when Mary greeted her.

And Mary said:
"My soul magnifies the Lord,
And my spirit has rejoiced in God my Savior."
For He has regarded the lowly state of His maidservant;
For behold, henceforth all generations will call me blessed.
Luke 1:46-48

HIS NAME IS JOHN

The naming of a child was a big event and took place on the eight day when he was to be circumcised. Everybody thought that Elizabeth would name her child after her husband Zacharias, but when they asked her, Elizabeth told them that his name is John. Then the people asked also Zacharias about the name, but Zacharias could not talk, since the archangel Gabriel had made him mute, so he wrote the name on a tablet.

And he asked for a writing tablet, and wrote, saying, "His name is John." So they all marveled. Immediately his mouth was opened and his tongue loosed, and he spoke, praising God. Luke 1:63-64

John is the Forerunner, the one who goes first and prepares the way for the Lord. Elizabeth and baby John hid from the wrath of Herod, who was seeking to kill all the children 2 years and under, as he wanted to kill the new born Baby Jesus the King of the Jews. John was not harmed.

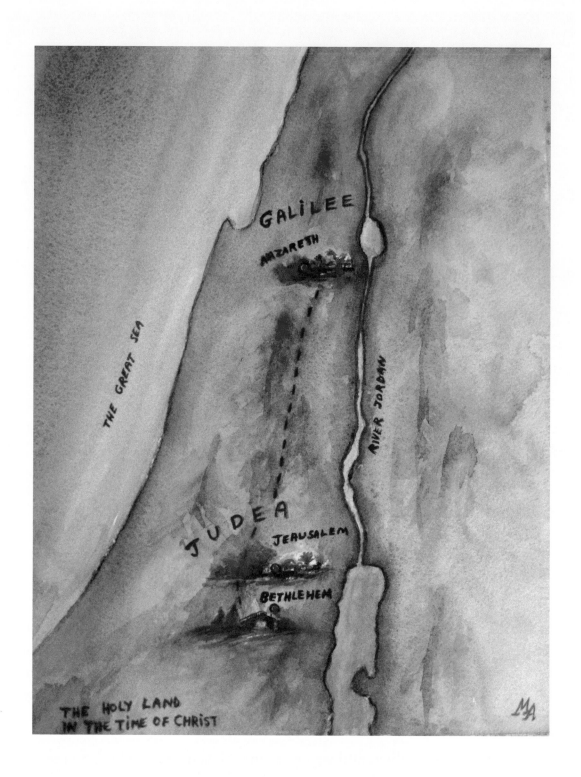

The Holy Land in the Time of Christ

BETHLEHEM THE CITY OF DAVID

At that time, the Roman Emperor Caesar Augustus ordered everyone to go to the city where they were born and register there, because he wanted to have a count of all the people in the places he had conquered and collect taxes from them. Joseph and Mary who lived in Nazareth of Galilee had to go to Bethlehem of Judea to register there, because Joseph was from Bethlehem, the City of David.

NO ROOM IN THE INN

It was a very long and tiring journey and the time was near for Mary to have the Baby. When they arrived in Bethlehem, the city was very crowded and they could not find a place to stay. Joseph was knocking on doors looking for a room to stay. But there was no room available. One of the inn keepers let them stay in the manger, a cave where they kept animals, and this is where Mary had Her Baby that Holy Night.

And she brought forth her firstborn Son, and wrapped Him in swaddling cloths and laid Him in a manger, because there was no room for them in the inn. Luke 2:7

SHEPHERDS ARE THE WITNESSES

That holy night Jesus was born in Bethlehem, the city of David. Shepherds were out in the fields at that time, watching their sheep, when suddenly with a bright light an angel of the Lord appeared before them. He was shinning and full of glory. When the shepherds saw him they fell on the ground with fear.

THE GOOD NEWS

Then the angel said to them, "Do not be afraid, for behold, I bring you good tidings of great joy which will be to all people. For there is born to you this day in the city of David a Savior, who is Christ the Lord. And this will be the sign to you: You will find a Babe wrapped in swaddling cloths, lying in a manger." Luke 2:10-12
Good news means Evangelion in Greek and in English Gospel.

MULTITUDE OF ANGELS

And suddenly there was with the angel a multitude of the heavenly host praising God saying:

"Glory to God in the highest,
And on earth peace,
Goodwill toward men!" Luke 2:13-14

Then the angels suddenly disappeared. They left and went back to heaven and the shepherds said to one another, "Let us go quickly and find this new born Child!"

HOLY NIGHT IN BETHLEHEM
ADORATION OF THE SHEPHERDS

The shepherds ran and found the Manger with Mary and Joseph and the Baby Jesus, and when they saw Baby Jesus they fell down and worshipped Him.

Then the shepherds returned, glorifying and praising God for all the things that they heard and seen, as it was told them. Luke 2:20

THE WISE MEN FROM THE EAST

Now after Jesus was born in Bethlehem of Judea, in the days of Herod the king, behold, wise men from the East came to Jerusalem, saying, "Where is He who has been born King of the Jews? For we have seen His star in the East and have come to worship Him." Matthew 2: 1-2

Herod the king was not glad to hear about another king. He told the wise men to return and tell him where this new King is, so he also can go and worship Him. Herod did not want to worship the new King of the Jews but he wanted to find Him and kill Him. The wise men left after they heard Herod. The bright star that was leading them from the East appeared again in the sky. They followed the star until it came and stopped on top of the manger where Baby Jesus was.

THE ADORATION OF THE WISE MEN

And when they had come into the house, they saw the young Child with Mary His Mother, and fell down and worshiped Him. And when they had opened their treasures, they presented gifts to Him: gold, frankincense, and myrrh. Matthew 2:11

The wise men did not go back to tell Herod where Baby Jesus was, but returned to their own country from another way, because an angel warned them in a dream not to tell Herod because he wanted to harm the Baby.

BABY JESUS IN THE TEMPLE

Simeon was a just and devout man from Jerusalem. He was waiting for the Savior of Israel. The Holy Spirit was upon him and had revealed to him that before he would die he would see Lord's Christ. Simeon led by the Holy Spirit was there on the day when Joseph and Mary brought Jesus to the Temple. Simeon recognized Baby Jesus as the Savior and the Messiah they all were waiting. When he saw Him he took Him in his arms, blessed God and said:

"Lord, now You are letting Your servant depart in peace, according to Your word; for my eyes have seen your salvation which you have prepared before the face of all peoples, a light to bring revelation to the Gentiles, and the glory of Your people Israel. Luke 2: 29-32

RETURN TO NAZARETH

An angel of the Lord appeared to Joseph in a dream after the wise men left and told him to take Baby Jesus and His Mother Mary and escape to Egypt and stay there until he gets another warning, because Herod would seek the Child to kill Him.

Joseph immediately took Jesus and His Mother Mary and left for Egypt that night. When Herod was dead, an angel of the Lord appeared to Joseph again in a dream in Egypt and told him to take the young Child and His Mother and go back to the land of Israel. They came back to Galilee and settled in the city Nazareth.

And he came and dwelt in a city called Nazareth that it might be fulfilled which was spoken by the prophets, "He shall be called a Nazarene." Matthew 2:23

JESUS OF NAZARETH

Jesus grew up in the house of Joseph, who was the protector of the Holy family, with the tender care of His Mother Mary, and He had wisdom and the Grace of God was upon Him.

So all this was done that it might be fulfilled which was spoken by the Lord through the prophet, saying: "Behold, the virgin shall be with child, and bear a Son, and they shall call His name Immanuel," which is translated, "God with us." Matthew 1:22-33

GLORY TO GOD

Angels in heaven and people on earth
Are singing praises to the Lord!

Glory to God in the highest, and on earth peace,
goodwill toward men! Luke 2:14

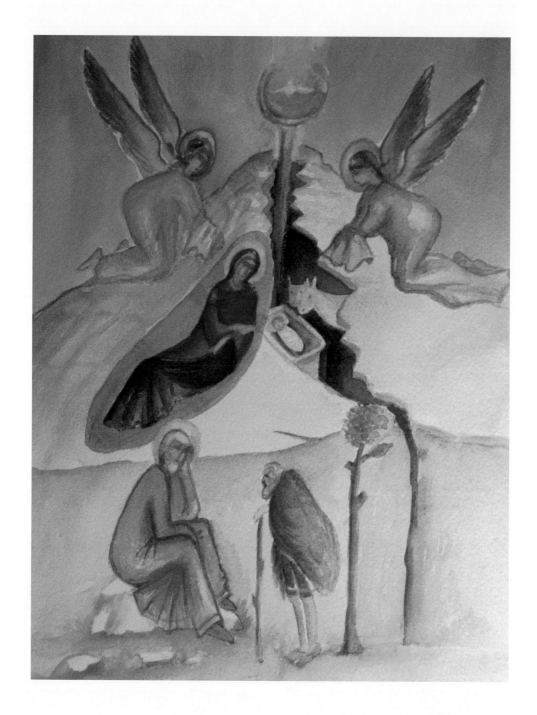

December 25 is Christmas Day, the holiday when the Church is celebrating the Nativity according to the flesh of our Lord and Savior Jesus Christ. It is a time of supreme joy and thanks giving to God for His amazing love and His amazing gift. Jesus gave us the gift of life and salvation and He is the ultimate gift!

Printed in the United States
By Bookmasters